SHEEPLESS NIGHTS

SHEEPLESS NIGHTS

LES KARAMAZOV

THE UNSLEEPERS' COMPANION

Elm Tree Books London

Edited by Richard McBrien

Designed by Kate Hepburn

Sheep drawings by Jon Riley
Artwork by Robyn Fairweather
Photos by Valerie Scott

© 1986 G.N. & R. Planer

First published in Great Britain 1986
by Elm Tree Books/Hamish Hamilton Ltd
27 Wrights Lane London W8 5TZ
British Library Cataloguing in Publication Data

Karamazov, Les
Sheepless nights: fun for one at three a.m.
I. Title
828'.91409 PN6175

ISBN 0–241–11965–0

Printed in Great Britain by Redwood Burn Ltd
Trowbridge, Wiltshire
Typesetting by Front Page Graphics, London

Biography

Les Karamazov has been awake since 1973. A fitful sleeper from his early youth, he first became aware of his particular gift when as a student he managed to stay awake through a whole side of a Leonard Cohen LP. Encouraged by this initial success he became interested in the whole phenomenon of sleeplessness and went on to remain alert through The Carpenters, Trollope, Barbara Cartland, The Eurovision Song Contest and more recently James Joyce. This year he hopes to stay conscious through the Prague Puppet Theatre's production of Chekov's Three Sisters, his most challenging attempt to date.

He worked his way through college with a number of jobs varying from newspaper boy to night-watchman; as a part time air traffic-controller he was dismissed for his general placidity and lapses of concentration. He graduated in social sciences from either Durham or Harvard University in 1975 and has now found a useful niche for his unusual talents running a small chain of twenty-four-hour launderomats.

In 1984 Les founded the Institute for Unsleepers, a registered Charity which now has over 1,200 non-sleeping partners. He launched the Institute in style by oversleeping and missing the inaugural address, thus breaking his eleven year old habit as an unsleeper. As he was heard to say later: "What address?" Les' ambition is to fall asleep free fall parachuting. He has been married to a gym instructor for several years and they hope one day to sleep together.

Introduction

Sleeplessness is a major problem of our time. More people stay awake from this one cause than any other. The inability to sleep, or *staying awake* as we doctors call it, has serious repercussions in every sphere of life. It causes stress, anxiety, unpleasant bags under the eyes and, paradoxically, sleepiness – at the wrong time. Victims can thus find themselves dropping off while driving, talking to the boss or making love – and possibly all three at once. It has been estimated that 83% of divorces are directly related to extra-nocturnal somnolence, or dozing. What, then, can modern science do to alleviate this? The answer is simple: nothing.

However, recent studies have revealed an ancient body of knowledge that is bringing hope to thousands of insomniacs. The idea is simple, almost absurdly so: sheep. Yes, sheep. Once the secret is revealed one feels one knew it all along. Who hasn't counted sheep to sleep? But that is just the tip of the iceberg. Sheep, it seems, naturally bring on sleep. Why this should be so has so far eluded extensive medical research, although recent work on Transpositional Theory is looking promising (sheep is sleep with an *h* instead of an *l*).

But who cares how it works. What is important is that it does – as this book will prove. For the first time collected between two covers is all the aspiring sleeper need know about sheep. From the purile to the profound, *Sheepless Nights* has rounded up the wisdom of the ancients and presented it in a form guaranteed to bring on sleep. No longer need you toss and turn, smoke ten cigarettes or dose yourself up with Valium. The ancient art of Sheeping is now available to all and slumber is just a few pages away.

If you can't sleep at 4am
put this book under your pillow and turn over

(not the book, idiot, turn over in bed)

Contents

I
Early Birds

You could be watching telly but have decided
on an early night.

II
Night Owls

You really should be asleep now.

III
Tossers & Turners

This is turning into an all-nighter.

IV
Headbangers

You're a pathological, hard-core insomniac;
just tense those muscles and wait for dawn.

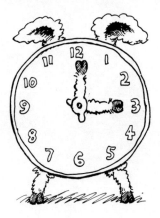

I
Early Birds

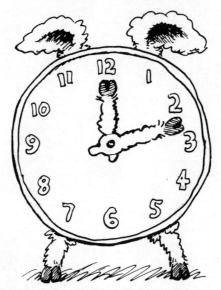

You could be watching telly but have decided
on an early night

Where did the term 'Counting Sheep' come from?

Counting sheep as a method of getting to sleep is known to most of us but what many do not realise is just how recent the idea is. Less than a hundred years ago the term was unknown.

At the height of the Victorian age, game shooting was widely practised not only by the upper classes but also by the ever-expanding middle class. Vast tracts of land were given over to grouse moors, huge areas of agricultural land turned over to shooting grounds. But even these massive efforts failed to meet the demand for the slaughter. And so the idea of the 'night hunt' was introduced. At first the hours were simply extended to eight or nine o'clock, but by the 1870s it was quite common to be potting quail up to midnight.

While this practice did alleviate over-crowding, it was not without its dangers. Increasingly hunters mistook colleagues, beaters and even spouses for prey with unfortunate results. The more enlightened estate owners strove to overcome the problem by introducing larger and therefore more visible game. After considerable experiment it was found that the humble sheep was ideal for the 'night hunt.' Not only was it large and white but rarely made any attempt to run away.

As sheep became more and more popular with the nocturnal stalkers it was found necessary to assign one sheep to one hunter and to this end sheep were given numbers painted onto their coats. It is here that we discover the strange linguistic slip that has given us the phrase 'counting sheep.' The gamekeepers, making their morning rounds, would invariably find the entire shooting party fast asleep with the sheep quarry contentedly nibbling the grass nearby. The late hour, combined with the strain of counting the sheep numbers and no doubt the victuals consumed before venturing out, brought on a profound sense of sleepiness. Hence the erroneous idea that counting sheep helps one to sleep. Incidentally, sheep hunts were banned by special Act of Parliament in 1910 after determined lobbying by Lady Barbara Ewing on behalf of the Cruelty in Cooking League.

SHEEPWORD

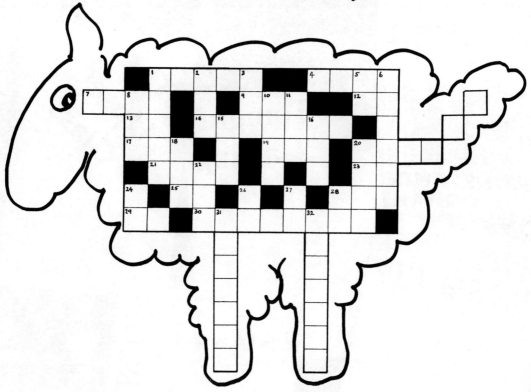

Across

1) What you'd like to do now
2) What d'you think of it so far?
7) A handful of sheep is worth two in this
9) Not a sheep, idiot
12) Your, his, our, their,
13) Ayiee!
14) ... tonight, tonight, tonight, tonight...
17) A quick one in the wee hours
19) The ugly woman's weapon for the fray
20) Roast lamb in the seat
21) Gasp at underwear
23) Mantra for stutterers
25) Go sleep, two
28) A sheepist comment
29) Hello again it's ego
30) If a bottle leaks you're in it

Down

1) Pretty obvious
2) Not me, it's a sheep
3) Come back to mine, softly
5) In the morning, I exist
6) Half of what you're wearing
8) A little taste of Mississippi
10) The cheeky get it
11) The cheeky get it for trying this
15) Tied up? Where's Kay?
16) Turn the lights on and I'll think about it
18) It's not tea, you're hungry
20) Going up, but it'll hurt a bit
22) Not the Japanese performing!
24) I exist, in the morning
26) Eureka; Information Technology!
27) Thanks Guv
28) I exist, in my Bonnett
31) Of dreams or on them
32) Turning to sing

WILD
NIGHTS

CONSTANCE
NORAH

Not Tonight,
Darling

Ivor Edake

The
Upset
Glass

I.C. Water

WILL
HE SLEEP?

BETTY WONT

THE LIVING ROOM

SOPHIE AGIN

Mornin
Noises

Lydia Desbin

Toss and Turn

Eliza Wake

reading

Thoughts through the Night
Penny Forem

ANNE GUISH

We Fell Out of Bed
Eileen Dover

...NTDOWN TO DAWN

...l the Alarm Go Off?

Isabel Rung

Phrig O'Dair

Night Starvation

Keep the Lights Off
Elsie Wakes

The Squeaky Noise
Buster Spring

The lucky dip decision maker

or Should I go for a pee now
or will it wake me up later if I don't?

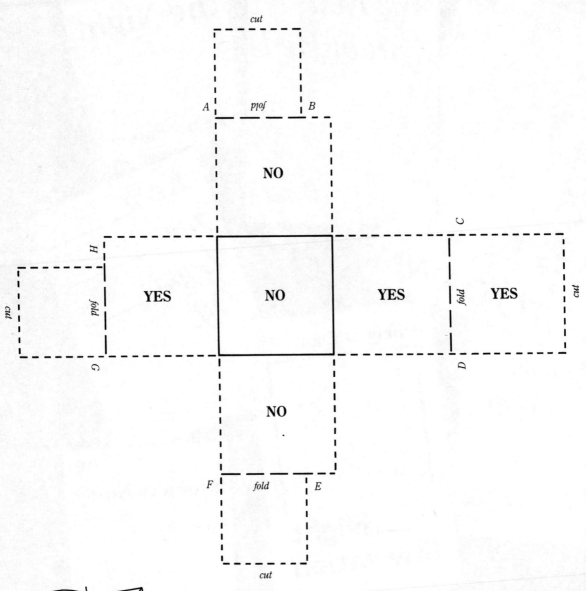

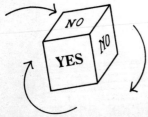

(continued from page 76) ... as the beads of sweat form on his back and the sides of his thighs. He clenched and unclenched his fist, a trick he'd picked up from his early days in the Service. His mind raced. He thought of the days ahead, of the months of hard work that had led up to them. He thought of the Ministry, of M, of the long summer evenings in the Club, he turned on his side, his Chinese silk pyjamas from Fortnums sticking to his perspiring flesh.

Through half closed eyes he watched a square of pale sunlight appear on the wall. A window, Dawn. He looked at his chunky Rolex, 5am. It had been a long night. He lay still, forcing his lungs to inhale slowly, rhythmically. He pretended to be asleep. Then it hit him. The sun was coming through the window! That meant the building must be facing North-East! K had been right all along. He made a mental note – the rear of the building must face South-West. The jigsaw was beginning to fit together.

Suddenly a noise beside him sent a shock wave of reaction through Bond's body. In a split second his training at Cheltenham came to him – he did nothing. He clenched his fist harder. The noise came again. Half gasp, half cough, Bond swallowed. Sounded like a woman. And close. Very close. He opened his eyes slowly. Very slowly. The wall. He was facing the wrong way. Bond turned over in the bed using the subterfuge of fifteen years. He opened his eyes. It was a woman all right. The hair, the face, the breasts, there couldn't be any mistake. He took the risk: "Are you awake?" "Yes" came the sighed reply. They'd got her too. Bond moved his hand... *(continued on page 36)*

The year of the Sheep

People born in the Year of the Sheep are characterised by a lack of individuality and commitment. They tend to follow others rather than risk standing out in a crowd. They rarely show initiative and have never been known to come up with a comment of their own.

Sheep people have a tendency to get stuck in the barbed wire of life and bleat helplessly until someone gets them out. They fall into emotional ditches and often fail to summon up the courage to climb out. They get snowed under by work and regularly die as a result.

Physically sheep people look remarkably similar, having rather silly faces and a lot of hair. They can be dirty and have the disconcerting habit of walking on all fours. However, they make ideal spouses and can be easily trained to do simple household chores. A dog usually keeps them in order.

Sheep colours are white and green. Their favourite pastimes are chewing the cud and looking stupid. Their idea of a good night out is freezing to death on a hill farm somewhere in Wales.

The insomniacs guide to watching TV

Make sure you are sitting on a seat where there is plenty of legroom. Preferably you should have a stool or table on which you can put your legs so that the old blood will return to the brain. There is nothing like having familiar blood in the brain to enhance that 'been here before' feeling.

Clasp the automatic channel changer loosely in your hand, sit back and start with a few quick easy channel hops. You might try:

Here is the news: 14 diplomats were today allowed to get their hands on Ewing Oil and I'm just not going to let them, do you understand, never, when you try Insta Baby potty pads so easy to discredit a proportional representation system.

then flip back the other way:

. . . this is his fourteenth try at the semi-finals and he's never loved you because he's not your real father and electro power, power that makes your home a discussion of the moral issues of natural childbirth, goodnight.

Carry on like this for half an hour or so until other people have left the room with headaches. Then you can either:

a) Switch off and get some hard earned rest.
b) Leave the set on until close down and then repeat as above.

(There is no need to stand up during the National Anthem as your blood will automatically return to your feet).

Les Karamazov's video choice

Still can't sleep? Why not try the real thing – Late Night Erotic Videos, reviewed here by yours truly Les Karamazov.

Erotique Bleux

Definitely my Number 1 choice this. A long (very long) French (or was it Czechoslovakian?) film with lots of dialogue, dozens of characters and virtually no action. Don't be put off by the photo on the cassette box of the woman removing her stockings. This scene lasts less than thirty seconds and is right at the end of the movie. Guaranteed to put you to sleep within the hour. I have yet to see the ending in thirteen attempts.

Two Way Double Swap Match

A close second. I'm still not sure what this one is about since it's been copied so many times you can't make out anything but blurred shapes. Maybe it's an Expressionist Erotic. Remember, it's always easier to fall asleep to a pirate video.

See You Later Elevator

An illuminating tale of a young lift operator whose call 'Going up!' is sometimes misunderstood, by the customers. This video works on the principle that repetition of a simple action is the most effective method of curing insomnia and proves that you can have too much of a good thing.

Six Virgins in Paris

Despite the promising title this film turns out to be about a group of Oxford athletes in the early nineteen hundreds. We follow them from their early days running along beaches in slow motion advertising sportswear to their unlikely triumph in the Olympics. Accompanied throughout by soporific music. A strange title but highly recommended, a yawn from beginning to end.(Are you sure the right tape was in the box? Ed.)

For the hard-core fans.

A horrible blob which kills by sucking brains through a straw. A story of unrequited stupidity with lots of teenagers in it.

THE THING

How an under-age American skateboarding teenager discovers his THING. What he does with his THING and how it gets eaten by a blob.

THE JELLY THAT ATE NEW YORK

A blob with a THING goes crazy in New York. Full cast of teenagers and THINGS.

A blob with a chain saw wreaks havoc in a DIY store. All teenage cast.

Small Ads

Which of the two sheep are identical?

An unknitting pattern

While away the hours twixt four and six unravelling this lovely pullover.

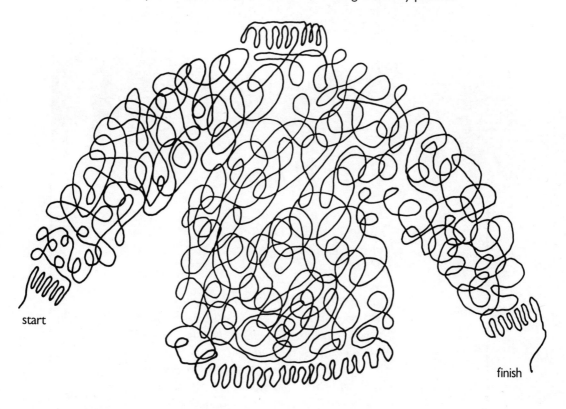

start

finish

Adding games

**Here is some simple arithmetic
for near mental cases at 4.17am**

1. Close your eyes
2. Pretend to be asleep
3. Worry
4. Now add the following together:

Visa balance
Bank balance
Milk bill
American Express
Mortgage for 19 years at 11.98%
School fees
Vets bills
Cost of painting bedroom
Next year's holiday
2 new suits
Medical insurance

‾‾‾‾‾‾‾‾‾‾‾‾‾‾‾‾‾‾‾‾‾‾‾

=

‾‾‾‾‾‾‾‾‾‾‾‾‾‾‾‾‾‾‾‾‾‾‾

− money in piggy bank

Grand Total =

‾‾‾‾‾‾‾‾‾‾‾‾‾‾‾‾‾‾‾‾‾‾‾

Night Thoughts

Oh what joy 'tis to recall
The merry Harvest Festival
How we skipped and jumped to see
The birds alight from budding tree
But you care not for that Summers day
Nor the merry warblings of the Popinjay
With heavy lidded eyes you yawn and cough
Too tired and drunk to turn the television off
And so I ramble on and on
About youth and Spring and ears of corn
Until with softened voice and laboured breath
I bore you all to sleep if not to death
And then I start talking about interesting things
Like sex and drugs and clotted cream
And then I do a Pixie dance around my chair
And tear out pages and stick them in my hair
And when of this I've had enough
I yell the single word 'FART!' . . . which wakes you up
But not believing it was me
You start and stare back at your screen
And seeing me talking once again
Of Harvest Festivals in Spring
You decide it must have been a dream
But if you're not sure that you were right
Sit up and listen again tomorrow night . . .

Pillow Talk

It's 2.00 on Tuesday morning, Sam and Susan are in bed talking
but their words have got muddled up.
Can you tell what they're saying?

Straight from the Doctor's Mouth

Insomniautokenesis

The human subconscious has long been the object of intensive scientific research and a good deal has been discovered. We now know, for example, that babies like their mothers and men and women are attracted to one another for psycho-sexual reasons. However, relatively little work has been done on the unconscious mind. Of course some members of the profession have been singing the praises of the unconscious state for some time – mostly as they are ejected into the gutter at 11.00. But now new research has revealed exciting new powers of this little-understood state. Powers of insomniautokenesis.

It seems that the semi-conscious mind of a person trying to sleep can have a physical effect on inanimate objects. This new power manifests itself not in hurling crockery and furniture about in altogether more subtle ways. It turns on electric appliances. It very slowly opens doors, creaks floorboards and eases on dripping taps. It rattles windows and doors and vibrates banisters.

Below is a room before and after a bout of insomniautokenesis. See if you spot the differences:

Famous Sheep Jokes....

What's woolly, got four legs and renowned for its stupidity?
A sheep (what did you expect? Some wise-arse political satire?)

If it takes four sheep eleven days to dig a hole, how long would it take them to dig half a hole?
There's no such thing as half a hole.

Catch that yawn

Help your own yawns along by matching these famous yawns
to their rightful owners:

1. Mick Jagger
2. Dracula
3. Bugs Bunny
4. The Queen
5. Frankenstein
6. Linda Lovelace
7. Hitler

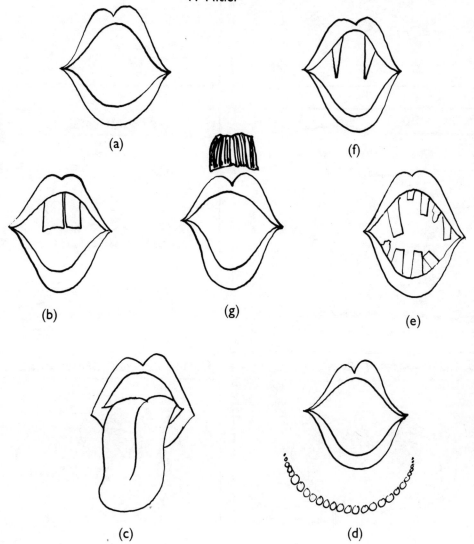

(a)

(f)

(b)

(g)

(e)

(c)

(d)

BED YOGA ....

1. THE MUMMY.

2. THE CRUMB.

3. THE HOG.

4. THE FORWARD ROLL.

5. THE REVERSE FORWARD ROLL.

6. THE DOUBLE SPRING ROLL.

7. THE BACKWARDS DOUBLE SPRING ROLL.

8. THE ULTIMATE SOLUTION.

9. THE REALLY ULTIMATE SOLUTION.

10. THE SECOND PILLOW.

11. THE FINAL REALLY ULTIMATE SOLUTION.

12. THE WALKABOUT.

Match that tune

Can you tell what tunes your alarm clock is tapping out?
Match the tic toc with the tune.

1. Tick tock tick tock tick tock tick tock

2. Tick tock tick tock

3. Tick tock tick tock tick tock tick tock tick tock tick tock

4. Tick tock tick

5. Tick tock tick tock tick tock tick tock tick tock

Criss Cross

**Can you find ten or more words to do with sheep
or even sleep, hidden in the box.**

D	L	P	T	S	D	G	B	S	T
R	O	F	O	H	R	Y	H	P	E
M	D	H	S	E	E	O	X	R	M
S	V	S	S	E	A	S	A	X	O
N	V	J	E	P	M	L	E	F	O
O	E	D	T	E	T	G	T	X	L
R	T	P	K	H	S	L	E	E	P
E	S	A	G	P	Y	J	A	M	A
L	W	I	N	I	G	H	T	E	Z
A	N	G	N	I	L	I	E	C	B

Sheepfinger

An unpleasant, but not contagious ailment, afflicting
some persons who have difficulty in sleeping at the
right time.

Manifestation:— see diagram; usually afflicts index
or forefinger; can occasionally infect all fingers of one,
or in rare cases, both, hands (see Flockfinger).

Causes:— Drumming with fingers on sides of bed late
at night. Aggravated by scratching at various parts of
the body – nose, ribs, head etc.

Symptoms:— Drumming with fingers on wood during
the daytime e. g. desks, kitchen units etc. after Rest
Deprivation.

Treatment:— Conventionally by steroid application to
finger(s) or, treating root cause, steroid application all
over patient. Alternative medicine advocates
symbiotic treatment (see Sheepdogthumb).

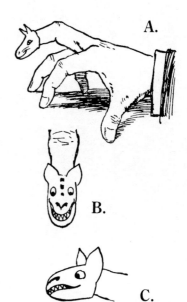

A.

B.

C.

II
Night Owls

You really should be asleep now.

Straight from the Doctor's Pencil Case

Anxiety

Anxiety is just another word for worry. I could have used metronome but that isn't another word for worry, so I didn't. This is called the scientific method.

Everybody worries and it is nothing to be worried about. I worry. In fact I worry quite a lot. I worry that I'm not making sense and then I worry that I do. It's a quite normal piece of behaviour found across all known cultures, like squeezing spots. The most important thing is: don't worry about worrying – it'll only make you worried and may give you spots.

Now many people worry about money. Most worry they haven't got enough of it but some people worry they've got too much. Fortunately for these people we have specialists who remove the money as fast as possible while the patient lies on his back relating his life history and being self-indulgent. In this way the worry is transferred to the doctor who can then dispose of it safely, usually in high-interest earning accounts and school fees.

Another common subject of worry is sex. Am I getting enough of it; am I doing it right; did I satisfy my partner; who is my partner? Men often worry unnecessarily about 'size'. Many's the time I've been asked, 'Dr, does size matter?' And I always give the same answer: Yes. A small willy just doesn't work.

If you do start worrying about something you can always remind yourself that things could be a lot worse. If this doesn't work try telling someone else your worries and they will invariably say: Things could be worse. The important point here is that things *could* be worse. For example you could go to a Greek restaurant, get a piece of kebab stuck in your throat and die horribly to the sound of balalaikas. Or the world could end tomorrow, which is probably much more worrying than the rather petty concern of being awake at four in the morning. After all, if these are your last hours, why waste them sleeping?

As a handy reference why don't you list the most worrying things you can think of below, then, when you're worried over something trivial just read the list and get really worried.

_____

_____

_____

_____

_____

_____

_____

_____

(Did that make any sense? Will I get paid for this? Who was that man with Susan last night? Has he got a bigger willy? How big is a big willy? How small is a small willy? Can I make a small willy into a big willy? Is this becoming a neurosis? Who cares about size? Does Susan care about size? Does Susan care about me? Do I care about Susan? Who is Susan? Who am I?)

Checklist

Susan is off to the big dream pastures but what has she forgotten?

Brush her teeth

Glass of water

Set the alarm

Put on pyjamas

Lock the back door

Answer: Worry about the Nature of Existence.

The sheep counter mobile

**The sheep counter mobile is an ingenious new sleeping aid
which you can make yourself! (patent expired 1876)**

Instructions

1.
a) Unwind a coat hanger
and make this shape.

2.
b) Bend another coat hanger
into this shape.

3.
c) Attach coat hanger
a) to coat hanger b) with string.

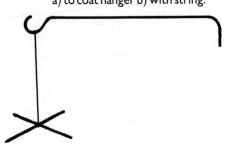

4.
d) Cut out sheep from page
and attach them with string
to coat hanger b)

6.
f) Count sheep as they pass
before your eyes;
soon you will be drowsy,
if not blow in opposite
direction.

5.
e) With belt or dressing gown cord,
tie mobile to head
and blow

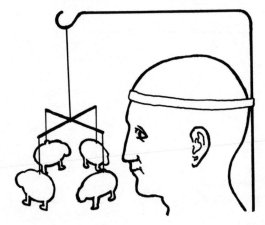

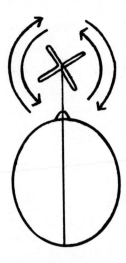

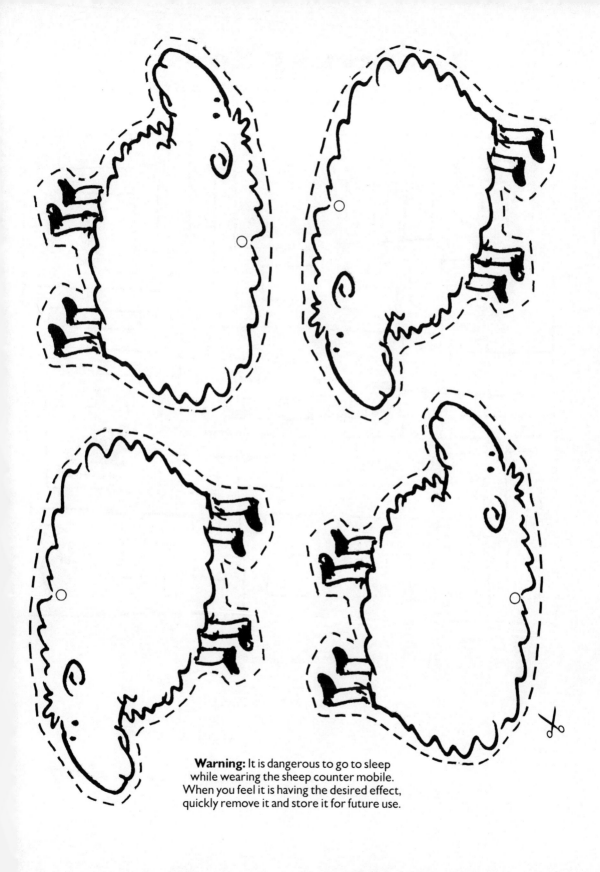

Warning: It is dangerous to go to sleep while wearing the sheep counter mobile. When you feel it is having the desired effect, quickly remove it and store it for future use.

The Creaky House

The burglar has to get to the middle of the maze, steal the money and cosh you;
but on the way he must also…

a) Step on the creaky floorboard
b) Tread on the cat
c) Knock over the broom
d) Help himself to the Scotch
e) Bang the bath tub…

(continued from page 20) ... over her long brown legs. She moved them further into the depths of the Belgian lace coverlet. The sheets felt cool and smooth against her, alleviating something of the ennui she felt so desperately. 'Strange' she mused 'how something cool can so soon become hot and passionate.' She stretched her lithe limbs, luxuriating in the suppleness of her young body. She ran a hand down her long smooth thighs. Her heart beat furiously, hammering at her breast. She felt sure James would hear it, would respond to the fire of her passion. She opened her large blue eyes and looked at him. He was asleep, suddenly, like a child.

She examined the clean cut face that was so dear to her. The rugged features looked almost boyish in sleep, the mask of manhood slipping to reveal the child beneath. Her heart went out to him and she wanted to snatch him to her breast, protect him from the evils of this world. She caressed his hair with her long sensitive fingers and thought of the first time they had met on that wind-swept cliff in France. He had called her name, she had turned and she knew immediately. They both knew. There was nothing to say. He furled his umbrella and they made long passionate love right there in the open, high on the cliff in the swirling rain. James later went down with influenza and she had nursed him through the long nights.

She eased her slender arm towards him, touching the muscular hair that covered his arm. He groaned in reply as she whispered into his ear "Cliff..." *(continued on page 54)*

Games Sheep Play :
Get Drunk and listen to Lionel Richie records

Pillow Talk II

It's 2.45 and Sam and Suzie are having another talk.
Can you sort out what they're saying?

Boring things to do

The secret to going to sleep is boredom and
here are some really boring things
to do to help you:

Try to go to sleep
Try again
Listen to the Shipping Forecast
Count the hairs on your body
Divide the number by six
By five
By four
Stare at the ceiling without blinking
Blink if you like
Try to remember every affair you ever had – in alphabetical order
Imagine making breakfast tomorrow
Think of 363 words beginning with *P*
Make an anagram of: I wish I could get to sleep
Try to remember exactly what you did ten minutes ago
See if you can spot any trains in your room
Pretend to be a stone
Pretend not to be a stone
Dribble
Hum Leonard Cohen songs
Try to think backwards
Put your finger in your ear
Take it out
Pretend to be asleep
Start again

Famous Sheep Jokes…. Famous Sheep Jokes….

Why did the sheep cross the road?
Dunno.
To get his reward. Geddit?
No.
Nor did the sheep.

Why is a sheep big, woolly and four legged?
Because if it was small, sleek and two legged it'd probably be a bird.

What do sheep have that no other animal has?
Baby sheep.

Knock knock.
Who's there?
Baaa.
Baaa who?
Baadaminhoff. Kabooom!

I say I say I say.
What do you say?
My sheep has no nose.
How does it smell?
Jamaica.

The Wakists

The Wakist movement was started by William Wakeham, a self-taught scholar and night-watchman in 1721. Bedevilled by a congenital ability to stay awake unnecessarily, William was granted a vision one Monday morning at 4 am. As he later wrote in his 'Letters to the Wakeful':–

> "The night was long and sore did I wish to close mine eyes and sleep. But then the Lord did appear unto me and said, verily: 'William! William!' whereupon I saith unto him: 'That be me.' 'William, William. Thou wert born to wake,' saith the Lord. 'Oh' saith I. 'Verily,' saith the Lord, 'thou shalt go forth and wake the world for this is my will and it shalt be done. For wherefore should my servant William be awake when all others doth sleep? Wherefore is the fun in that? They shall wake too!' Whereupon I fell down in a fit of wakefullness and have not shut mine eyes since that day."

Armed with his holy injunction William founded his movement. At first restricted to waking schoolboys who dozed at their desks or labourers grabbing forty winks in the local public house, the movement soon grew to embrace afternoon naps and shortly any extra-curricular sleeping.

However, it was with his extension into night time that William began to be perceived as a true radical. Ignoring the local preference to sleep at night, and not a few threats, William proceeded to keep his village (Tossington in Bedfordshire) awake the whole night through by banging hazel twigs on an empty firkin. While his ingenious justifications did hold some water (he pointed out that the National Debt could be paid off in five years if people would only work 24 hours a day) they were mostly not appreciated and William was expelled from Tossington in 1723.

Thus began the Wakists' darkest hour. With membership stubbornly refusing to rise above one, the Society was forced to wander from village to village searching for converts. It was not an easy period and success could only be described as minimal. Indeed, by 1724 William was quite disheartened and not a little tired. He wrote in his memoirs 'Awake and Onwards':–

> "Mine eyes were verily heavy and my brain did throb. Verily were it not for my faith in the calling, verily I believe I would have succumbed to the false comfort that men call sleep. Verily."

It was here, in the moment of his despair that William met the man who was to change his life: Harvey Cushioner. Cushioner, a Puritan preacher who believed that heavenly bliss was the reward for earthly discomfort, took to the philosophy of Wakism immediately. It was Cushioner who persuaded William to abandon the old world for the new and to set sail for the Americas. Almost as the news was announced popularity seemed to follow and the previously scorned movement was granted a Royal Charter the minute the King heard of its proposed departure.

> "... our plefure on their departing marred only by our concern left day return ticketf be introduced. Neverthelef we, GR, in our absolute mercy allow faid Wakifts to make a journey of a ufeful and ferious fature for fuff fif finff fly fof fum funny fy fluff ..."

The two hopefuls set sail for Chesapeake Bay in 1726 and The New World proved a fertile land indeed for the Society. Within three years the Wakists had over four members and by the end of the decade the number had swelled to seven, covering most of New York, New England and territories around Virginia. The combination of Puritanical severity, bad neighbourliness and unending noise proved irresistible. Village after village was woken in the early hours and converted to misery.

The Society prospered and in the climate of enquiry and practicality that characterised the age, applied for a licence to manufacture artefacts for sale. These artefacts were, as defined in the Letters of Patent, to be produced by members between the hours of two and five am. The charter went on to limit both the noise that the Wakists could make and the candlepower they might use. On the face of it the restrictions of "no noyse, no light and no leaving of the bedchamber" left little room for manoeuvre. However, a strong sense of resourcefulness and many hours of spare time allowed the Wakists to invent ingenious ways round the limitations; Wakist artefacts showed astonishing attention to detail and rapidly became collectors items.

Figure 1 shows a Wakist pencil with characteristic 'dog tooth' end, probably produced with the teeth.

Figure 2 shows a combined half-filled drinking beaker and handkerchief holder.

Figure 3 shows an extract from an uncompleted novel (less of an unfinished book, almost a religious totem for Wakists).

The movement was at its height in the late 18th and early 19th century but thereafter declined as the offspring of Wakists rebelled by snoozing and dozing openly and in public, much to the dismay of their parents. This, and the improvement in bed manufacture, gradually eroded membership until by 1850 the Wakists had all but ceased to exist. However, Wakist culture left a distinct mark on the Eastern seaboard of the USA, and any present day researcher trying to sleep, can still find reminders of the Society and its ever wakeful founder in the lively atmosphere of early morning New York.

The Water Wheel of Fortune

Cut out the spinner below, insert a matchstick and
decide what to do with that tumbler of water.

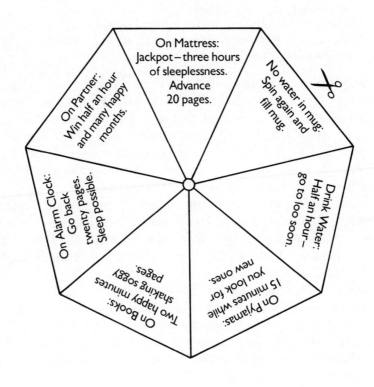

On Mattress:
Jackpot – three hours
of sleeplessness.
Advance
20 pages.

No water in mug:
Spin again and
fill mug.

On Partner:
Win half an hour
and many happy
months.

Drink Water:
Half an hour –
go to loo soon.

On Alarm Clock:
Go back
twenty pages.
Sleep possible.

On Pyjamas:
15 minutes while
you look for
new ones.

On Books:
Two happy minutes
shaking soggy
pages.

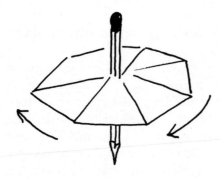

Practical tips for unsleepers

1 Wear sleeping tablets on a string round your neck. You can nibble them without getting up.

2 Cut a section of hosepipe about one and a half feet long to use as giant straw for water, Horlicks and other beverages.

3 Cut a section of hosepipe five feet long to hang out of the window to use after drinking water, Horlicks and other beverages.

4 Shave now and save time in the morning.

5 Staple sheets to the mattress to avoid wrinkled sheets.

6 Set alarm for 3am – since you always go back to sleep after it's gone off.

7 Go to bed dressed so you're ready to get up at a minute's notice.

8 Do housework.

9 Write indignant letters to the council complaining about the brightness of street lamps.

10 Phone Australia and talk to a sheep.

11 Write a list of things to do before going to sleep.

HOW TO MAKE A CUP OF TEA

00.20

1. CAN I BE **BOTHERED**? IS IT **WORTH** IT? I'LL PROBABLY JUST **NOD OFF** ANYWAY.

00.30

2. YES, A **CUP OF TEA** WOULD BE **NICE**. I THINK I'LL **DEFINITELY** GET MYSELF ONE IN A **MINUTE**.

00.40

3. **GET UP** AND **BUMP INTO THINGS** IN **DARK**. STUB **TOE**. SSSSSH!

00.45

4. **GO OUT** OF ROOM, DOWN **CORRIDOR**.(CREEP) FIND **DOOR HANDLE**. **OPEN** DOOR.

00.55

5. SWITCH ON **LIGHT**. OOPS **WRONG DOOR**. LEAVE **TOILET**. GO TO **KITCHEN**.

01.20

6 FIND **KITCHEN**. TURN ON **LIGHT**. LOOK FOR **TEA**. LOOK FOR **CUP** UNDER **WASHING UP**. **DO NOT** MAKE **NOISE** WITH **DIRTY CROCKERY**.

IN 2½ HOURS

01.50

7. FILL **KETTLE**. WAIT FOR IT TO **BOIL**.

02.05

8. SWITCH KETTLE **ON**. THIS TIME IT'LL **BOIL**.

02.15

9. POUR **TEA**. WAIT FOR IT TO **BREW**.

02.20

10. WAKE UP. POUR AWAY **COLD TEA**. MAKE **ANOTHER CUP**.

02.25

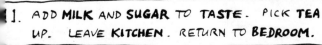

11. ADD **MILK** AND **SUGAR** TO **TASTE**. PICK **TEA** UP. LEAVE **KITCHEN**. RETURN TO **BEDROOM**.

02.50

12. STUB **TOE** ON **BED** AGAIN AND **SPILL TEA** OVER **BEDCLOTHES**.

Enjoy An Insomniac's Holiday

Club 22 to 4am offer you The Holiday of a Nightime for just £49.95

Can't sleep? Why stay at home being miserable when you can be twice as miserable on one of our specially tailored all-night tours!

Visit London, the most famous capital city in England. See places you never dreamed existed! We'll show you Londoners as they really are – warm, friendly and fast asleep. Then we'll let you wake them up. Watch as they become angry! Thrill as they turn aggressive!

The 'Are you looking at me, Jimmie?'

The Yah & Yawn

A night to remember

Our tour starts just as pubs close. Drink in the sounds and smells of a late night brawl outside the pub of your choice.

next, it's off to miss the last train from Waterloo. But don't worry – there are plenty of things to see and do on your walk through late-night London.

Under the bridge at Charing Cross station we visit London's homeless tramps, famous for their stories and cheerful hospitality.

*j*ust a few hundred yards
down the road we visit the Texas
24 Hours Service Station with its
dazzling neon Las Vegas style. It's
time to stock up on crisps, sweets
and key rings and while there why
not try the easy-to-enter Las
Vegas lottery and win yourself a
Pyrex wine decanter.

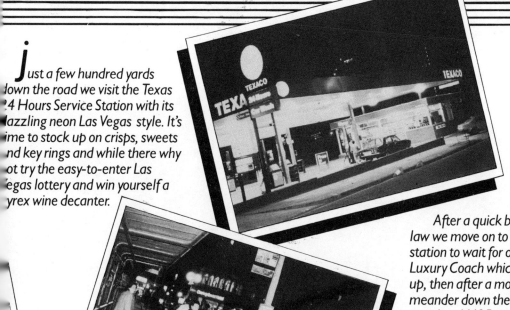

After a quick brush with the
law we move on to Victoria bus
station to wait for our Special
Luxury Coach which doesn't turn
up, then after a moonlight
meander down the lovely leafy
tree-lined M25 we arrive at
Heathrow's Terminal Four. Join
fellow tourists for an all-night vigil
in the airport lounge of the future.

Finally, no night in London
would be complete without a visit
to the Railway Cafe in Vauxhall to
watch the sun rise over a plate of
egg and chips. For no extra charge
Daisy will polish your shoes with a
broom.

Then we're off again to spot
the legendary Night Bus which is
rumoured to run from Central
London to Crouch End though
only a handful of locals claim to
have seen it.

Then, tired, unhappy and full
of the sights and sounds of the
night, it's back to sleep it off in the
luxurious comfort of your own
home.

*O*n, forever onwards.
Stopping off briefly to be refused
entry to Stringpersons famous
nightclub, we find ourselves at the
All-night Chemist in Wardour
Street. A mecca of social activity
where London characters meet to
watch the world go by and pick up
their prescriptions.

Club 22 to 4am reserve the right to
cancel this tour at short notice.

III
Tossers & Turners

This is turning into an all-nighter.

Wave book from side to side

Self-hypnosis

You are feeling sleepy. You are feeling sleepy. You are deeply relaxed and feeling very very heavy. Your left foot is perfectly relaxed. It is heavy and relaxed and warm. The whole of your left leg is now heavy and deeply relaxed, it feels part of the bed it is so relaxed. Now your right leg is deeply relaxed and numb, it is perfectly heavy. You are going to sleep. Your body is deeply heavy and perfectly numb, it is very relaxed. Your head is deeply perfect and heavily sleepy. Your right ear is perfectly relaxed and warm. Your left ear is deeply relaxed and itchy. Your nose is perfectly relaxed. Your left ear is still deeply relaxed and itchy. Your left foot is heavily relaxed and also itchy. Relax. Relax all your muscles. Your left foot is not at all itchy. Nor is your nose. Relax. Isn't it amazing how an itch just disappears. You are now in a state of deep, relaxed, perfectly heavy hypnosis. You are aware only of my voice. Now get out of bed and fetch your jacket. You are perfectly relaxed and warm. Now get back into bed. Good. You feel very sleepy. Now take out your cheque book and pen, good, and write out a cheque for £582.79 to:

Dr S. B. Karda and don't forget to post it tomorrow to: Pen 23b, Milton Keynes.

Good. You will forget all that I have told you except to post that letter. You are feeling sleepy, you are

feeling sleepy, you are drifting into a deep sleep, a perfectly deep and relaxing sleep . . . .

The best idea I ever had

It was three seventeen on a wintery morning in July as I lay awake counting the minutes to dawn (she likes it when I count to her). Time stood still, I did not. I tossed and turned, and then I moved about too. I lay on my side, my other side, on my back, on my front, my nearly right side, my nearly left side. I dozed, I dreamt. I lay on my face, I lay on my back, I stuck my feet out of the duvet. I pulled them back. I stretched out. I scrumpled up. I put my bum out of the duvet, in the duvet, over the duvet, under the duvet. I dozed, I dreamt. I turned over. I turned round, put my head at the bottom of the bed, at the top of the bed, the side of the bed, near my bum, far from my bum. I dozed, I dreamt. I put my hand over my eyes, in my hair, by my sides, between my legs. I held on, I let go, I moved up and down. I dozed, I dreamt. And then it came to me.

The problems of the country stood before me, the problems of the world stood before me, the problems of the entire universe stood before me. Clearly.

In a flash I understood it all. Everything. The lot. I had solved the problems of Mankind. I was All-Knowing. Quickly I reached for a pencil lest the vision slip away. Alas, there was no pencil. I looked for a burnt matchstick to etch my inspiration in charcoal. There was no match. Frantically I searched for a lipstick, a nail, a pin to preserve the Truth in my own blood. All in vain.

Exhausted by my efforts slumber overtook me (I hadn't even caught sight of it in my mirror). Dawn came and as usual woke me – she's not the silent type. Alas, alack the revelation was no more. The Gods had taken back their gift of knowledge and I was left with no more than a ravaged bedside table. Mankind must suffer on.

Moral: Keep a pencil and paper by your bed. Who knows, you might save the universe.

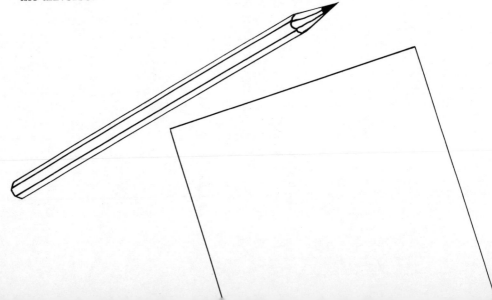

Word to Word

**See if you can turn these words into each other,
changing just one letter at a time.**

Here's an example: Bed → Eat.

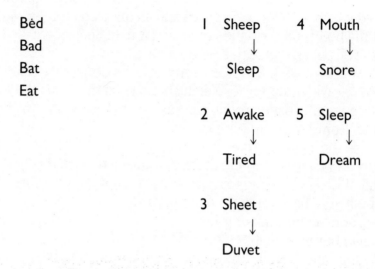

Bed
Bad
Bat
Eat

| 1 | Sheep ↓ Sleep | 4 | Mouth ↓ Snore |

| 2 | Awake ↓ Tired | 5 | Sleep ↓ Dream |

| 3 | Sheet ↓ Duvet | | |

Games Sheep Play:
Talking Hi-Fi

(*continued from page 54*) ... the oysters my Lord H had given me have given bad night's rest tonight and many times I waked and thought myself mightily bit with fleas. In the morning I will chide the maids for not looking the fleas a-days. But when I look I find none. Perhaps it is only a change in the weather from hot to cold which doth stop my pores and so my blood tingles and itches all time all over my body and continues to do so for many hours. Up and to the privy again which will put an end to this restlessness.

And so to bed. Thence to my wife's side who is sleeping mightily and I fondle her with thoughts of waking her and further. But she wakes not and I pull the lace counterpane around me since I am too cold now. It is a fine sheet and cost £5 from a friend of Mr Creeds.

Up and again to the little room which will be the last time this night. Methinks I have now found the proper place to lie in this bed which I got from a friend of Lady C. Would that she had accompanied it. I turn to thinking more of the Lady C, a fine woman and not unbuxom. And true I would have spent many a fine hour contemplating her image in my mind but for the shaking of the bedchamber by a mighty storm. The Lord doth see into my heart. It rains very hard, rain and hail that threatens the very foundations of my house and I do regret all that has passed between Myself and Lady C, though it be only a glance or two. I concern myself over the panes which cost more than £2 from Josh the glazier, but they take the beating well.

My eyes refuse sleep and I turn again to my sleeping wife, full of remorse for ungodly thoughts concerning Lady C. This night she has been in chagrin humour, my wife, and I doubt not that she is truly awake. But her stubbornness refuses to allow us mutual satisfaction and so I turn at last and to take a spoonful of Mr Batter's preparation, advised by Mr Hunt for just such occasion. This results in a visit once more to the privy and the production of two fine stools. This excellent performance puts me in fine humour and I return to tell my wife. We lie a while and so to up, and at once ... (*continued on page 20*).

Famous Sheep Jokes...

What is a sheep with a lamb called?
A mummy.

How many sheep does it take to change a light-bulb?
None: sheep don't have lights, stupid.

Join up the dots

Join up the dots to reveal a familiar four legged animal

(Answer on page 263)

Ways to wake your partner up

1. Deep sighs
2. Coughing
3. Advanced coughing
4. Throw bedclothes on floor
5. Fart (may need preparation)
6. Throw bedclothes on partner and complain
7. The Little Cuddly Wuddly (don't get carried away)
8. Thrash around in throes of traumatic nightmare
9. Wet bed
10. Switch on light and read Wordsworth
11. Switch on light and recite Wordsworth

Careful combinations of the above may prove effective,
for example wetting the bed while having a nightmare
can elicit sympathy. However, commonsense should be observed.
Do not, for instance, attempt (7) after (5).

You can win £10,000,000 in our easy to enter Sheep Dip! Just think what you could do with all that lovely loot! You could replace that broken window or buy yourself a new pair of slippers and still have enough over to bail out the Third World country of your choice!
Here's how to enter our easy competition. It's as simple as ABC. Just fill in the boxes below and send off the completed form to: Sheep Dip, Pen 34, Milton Keynes.

Win £10,000,000!!!!!

What letter begins the alphabet? _____

What letter comes next? _____

What letter is before D? _____

Name: _____

Address: _____

_____

Can we use your name in our publicity? _____

And now just complete the following in not more than twelve words:

'Is life simple or complicated? _____

And the first correct entry out of the hat wins **£10,000,000!!** Hurry, it could be you!

What to say to your partner when you've woken them up

1. (Deep sigh) 'Nothing, dear.'
2. (Cough) 'It'll go in a minute.'
3. (Advanced cough) 'You couldn't get me some tea, could you?'
4. (Covers on floor) 'You did it.'
5. (Farting) 'You did it.'
6. (Throw covers at partner) 'You've done it again.'
7. (Cuddly wuddly) 'Oh, I only wanted a cuddle – don't get carried away.'
8. (Nightmare) 'Aaaaaaaaaagh! Uuuuuuuugh! Oooooooooooooh!'
9. (Wet bed) Sssssssssss.
10. (Reading Wordsworth) Say nothing.
11. (Reciting Wordsworth) 'I wandered lonely as a cloud…'

Uncle Sam's Pet Corner

Well, it's Spring again and the time of year when people are thinking of buying pets. This year why not try a sheep? These delightful creatures make ideal pets, requiring the minimum of attention, just ¾ acre of good quality grazing and the occasional sheep dip. Who can resist those frisky little lambs? But a sheep isn't just a beauty to behold, it is also fun to play with and an asset to any house.

If trained from an early age a sheep can be taught all sorts of fun tricks, like ignoring thrown sticks or falling into ditches. You can even get him to obey the 'stay' command – for anything up to eight days! And of course your pet also has a more serious side, he'll loyally protect your property from encroaching grass, stare down hostile intruders and even catch slow-moving rats.

All-in-all the sheep is the perfect pet: loyal, reliable and loving. For just a few pence a day you can enjoy his many moods. And if you should become a bit bored just slit his throat for a tasty Sunday lunch.

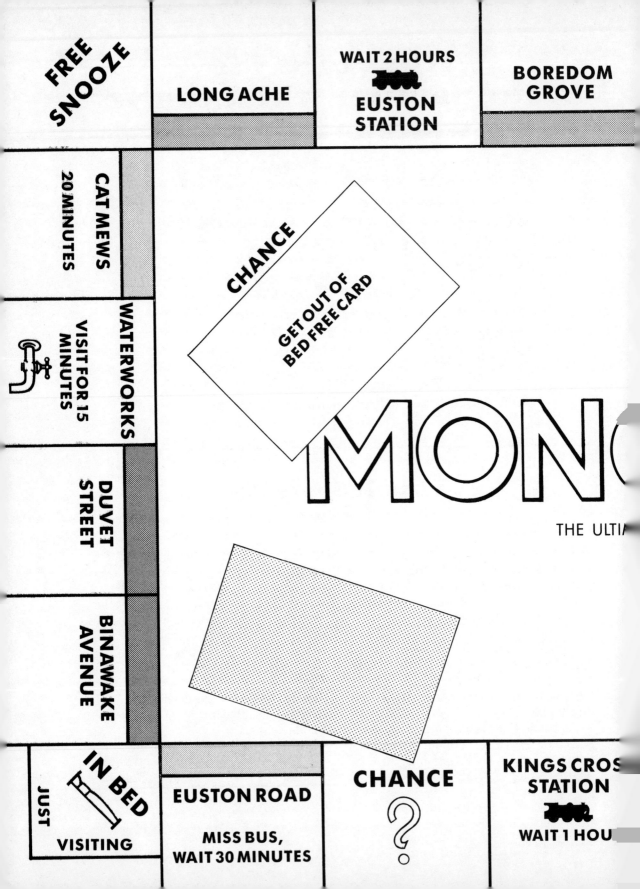

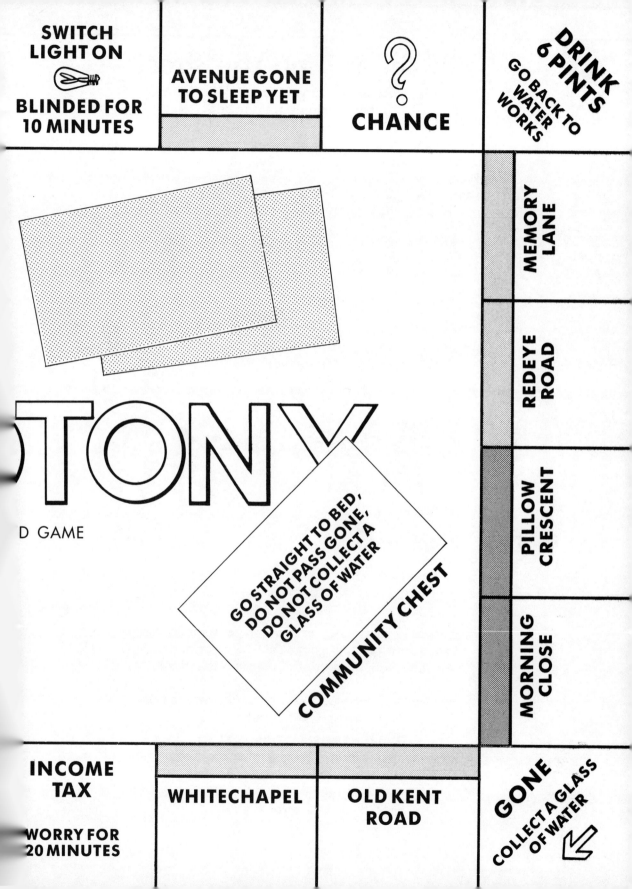

Pin the tail on the sheep

**Here's a fun game you can play for hours
in the comfort of your bed.**

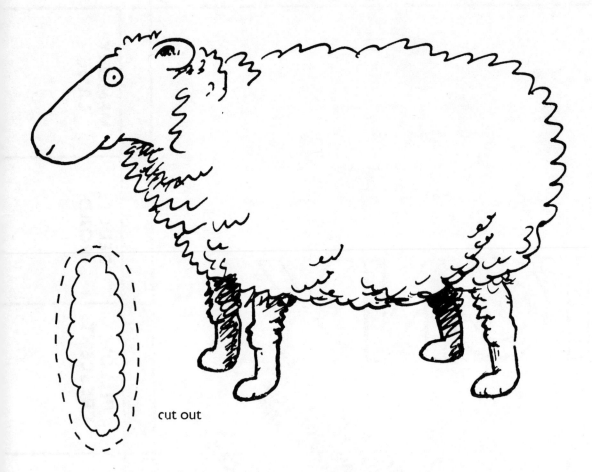

cut out

Just cut out the tail (sorry, you'll have to get some scissors, ed.).
Now, put the pin through the tail (sorry, you need a pin).
Shut your eyes and stick the pin in the sheep.

Well done! That was fun, wasn't it? Now we can play a
variation on the same game:

Pin the sheep on your partner

This time shut your eyes and try to pin the sheep on your
partner where you think they would most like it.
Don't worry if you get it wrong, they'll soon wake up
and tell you where you can stick it.

Famous Faces

Here's how to do it:

1. Lie flat on your back with only one small pillow and your head well back.

2. Relax.

3. You're still tense. Relax some more. Breathe abdominally four times.

4. Stare hard at the ceiling for two minutes. Try to avoid blinking.

5. Suddenly the magic shadow paints will begin to work. A host of famous faces, past and present will parade before your eyes. There goes Napoleon with Vivien Leigh. Pinocchio! And there's Julius Caesar (from the side) and who's that? Cinderella on a skateboard and look, Winston Churchill with the body of a frog. (Well, it is if you make Pinocchio's nose the cigar and Napoleon's hat the frog's bottom.)

Famous Faces Part II
Roll over onto your side and repeat.

Famous Faces Part III
Roll over onto your other side and repeat.

Famous Faces Part IV
Tell your sleeping partner about it.

How to use this book

put left eye
here

put nose here

to really get to sleep

put right eye
here

Pillow Talk III

It's 3.30 on Tuesday morning and Sam and Suzie are
still in bed and are having another conversation.
Can you help them sort it out again?

Small Ads

SAMUEL SMYTHE'S SNORE-SOOTHER

The gentleman of taste cannot afford to travel without Samuel Smythes Patented Snore-Soother. This beautifully produced mechanism ensures that even the most voluble of snorers will be silenced. Indispensable when travelling in mixed company, the Snore-Soother is guaranteed to turn the most manly of snores into a gentle purr, suitable, even, for the ears of the fairer sex.

Available from superior suppliers of surgical appliances. Also available: Samuel Smythes' Flatulence Silencer.

OVER-NIGHT-SUCCESS

Make up to £5,000,000 overnight! Sounds incredible? Thousands of ordinary people have achieved this and more! "At 9pm I was unemployed, by morning I was a multi-millionaire!" T. Anderson, Teddington. "It really works – I'm rich!" G. Anderson, Tadcaster. Amazing new money-making idea guarantees instant wealth. No selling involved. Start getting rich tonight! "I want to be a millionaire in 24 hours. Please rush me your foolproof system. I enclose £23.73 plus £17 p+p" Mail to: H. Anderson, Over-night-Success, Pen 1, Milton Keynes.

LADIES? BETWEEN 18 & 30? WORRIED ABOUT MONEY?

Can't sleep at night? Anxious about money? Why not make good use of those long, lonely hours by becoming one of our highly-paid homeworkers? Work from the comfort of your own bed and watch the money pile up. No training necessary – instant start. Just lie back and think of England. Phone Mick at Dial-a-Bit for full details. You could be earning tonight.

FOR SALE

Partner: little used. Charming, intelligent, sexually active. References available. Divorce forces sale. Possible swap for 35hp speed-boat.

KNOW YOUR FUTURE

Experienced clairvoyant tells your future by reading dirty sheets. Don't be in the dark, send soiled linen to Madam Zabuska, Pen 56, Milton Keynes.

SLEEP YOUR WAY SLIM

Lose up to 50lb overnight. Amaze your friends, stun your relatives, become a completely new person with new *Sleep-it-off*. It doesn't matter if you're overweight, fat or a real slob, this new wonder-drug from Sweden will turn you into a beautiful sylph overnight. Just take 3 tablets before retiring. Dissolves flab instantly. *(Government Health Warning! Do not use this product).*

FEET HEAT and HOW TO CURE IT

The Patented Summer Foot Cooler

Unfortunately the feet are too far away from the mouth to benefit from the relief which might be afforded by blowing, so the 'Summer Foot Cooler' has been devised for the discerning sleep enthusiast.

SLEEPY-CLOCKS

The last word in hi-tech time-keeping. Designed in W. Germany and built in Japan, the Sleepy-Clock uses the latest state-of-the-art electronics. Just attach the sensors to your wrists before retiring and the Sleepy-Clock will automatically monitor the state of your body. As soon as you drift off into a doze the Sleepy-Clock emits an ear-shattering 185 decibels of alarm to wake you up again. Also available with 500 volt electric-shock probes for silent operation. Send for details.
Pen 76

SLEEP-O-GRAM

The perfect gift for the insomniac who has everything. Over twelve really boring characters to choose from, including: the computer buff; the train spotter; the SDP candidate and DIY enthusiast. Boredom is just a phone call away! *324 8634*

RADIO BREAKTHROUGH

Fully portable short-wave radio for under £50! This hyper-sensitive receiver lets you pick up programmes from all over the world. Thrill to Albanian peasant songs, laugh at Korean sit-coms, learn from the news in Serbo-Croat. A faithful companion through the night. Complete with batteries and universal dictionary. Available at Boots and good chemists.

What happens to your body when you go to sleep

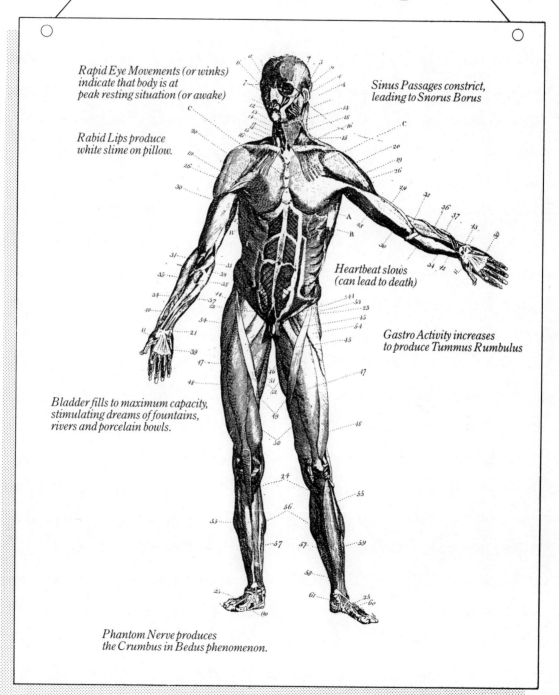

Rapid Eye Movements (or winks) indicate that body is at peak resting situation (or awake)

Rabid Lips produce white slime on pillow.

Sinus Passages constrict, leading to Snorus Borus

Heartbeat slows (can lead to death)

Gastro Activity increases to produce Tummus Rumbulus

Bladder fills to maximum capacity, stimulating dreams of fountains, rivers and porcelain bowls.

Phantom Nerve produces the Crumbus in Bedus phenomenon.

IV
Headbangers

You're a pathological, hard-core insomniac;
just tense those muscles and wait for dawn.

Straight from the Doctor's Bed

Dreams

Dreams, what are they and what are they for? These are questions which have plagued Man since the beginning of the week. A dream, said Freud, is a message from the subconscious to the id, but who was he and what did he mean? Why send a message in a dream? If you've got something to say why not just come out with it face to face, or at least phone?

Dreams can tell us a lot about ourselves. I, for instance, discovered that I am a handsome genius from a dream. They also contain images and symbols which if interpreted correctly can reveal hidden depths. Thus if you dream about missing a train and getting to work late this does not mean that you are worried about missing your train and getting to work late. No. It means your father was dominant, your mother was over protective and you often felt they didn't understand you. The station, of course, represents the womb, or perhaps death, or maybe a craving for cheesecake. The train symbolises the male, with its phallic shape and ejaculatory steam (if electric this shows repression of sexuality). If you are a man this means you want a bigger member, if you are a woman this also means you want a bigger member, since everybody secretly wants a bigger member more than anything else.

Some people suffer from recurring dreams which can be very disturbing or, if they feature prolonged sexual intercourse, worth staying in for. Sometimes I go to sleep just on the off-chance that I'll have one of these. Then there are nightmares, in which the id and the ego battle it out until you wake up screaming. A typical nightmare might be that you dream everyone is whispering behind your back and nobody likes you. This is a perfectly normal 'paranoic' dream, and simply means that people have difficulty getting on with you and feel the need to tell each other about it behind your back.

Another extremely common dream scenario is that of being tied to an olive tree by seven female Viking warriors who cover your body in Bacofoil and feed you dried bananas and anchovies. With the average person, this dream should recur once or twice every two or three days. At least it does with me.

Games for two

**Generally insomnia is a solitary pastime
but if you're lucky enough to be part of an insomniac couple
there are lots of games you can play à deux.**

1) Pretend to be asleep so well that your partner really thinks you are. This is much more fun if they play too. Really ham it up: deep breathing, snores, sudden starts, that sort of thing, The winner is the one who *doesn't* ask: "Are you awake?"

2) Pass the parcel – with a difference! Wrap a household object in tin foil and place at the bottom of the bed. Each player then tries to remove a layer with their feet.

3) Find the right position (for sleeping only).

4) Pull the bedclothes off.

5) Start up an argument your partner thought had finished weeks ago.

6) Play I-Spy with your eyes shut.

7) Guess the time: one partner calls out the time, the other turns the light on to check.

8) Pick each other's noses.

9) See how many words you can make out of: I wish I could get to sleep.

10) Repeat: 'Sleep Deep Sweet Sheep' until one of you makes a cup of tea.

11) A brain teaser! Sam is five years older than Suzie but for the last ten years Suzie has only slept three-quarters of the time Sam has. How long will it be before Suzie looks as old as Sam?

12) Make a list of why you don't like each other.

Games Sheep Play:

Wearing trousers that are too tight

Follow that dream

"If you want to know what you're really like, look in the mirror" said Zarathrusta in the famous play. But ever since Freud discovered hormones, people have wanted to explore their personalities the scientific way – through dreams.

Dreams of course are a direct line to your subculture and so we asked a famous chiropractor to design a simple psycho-quiz so you can discover more about yourself. The game is easy – we supply the Dream So Far and then you must tick the box that gives the answer closest to how *your* dream would probably work out. Add your scores up from the ticked boxes and read off your personality from the chart at the bottom of the page. Go on – and be honest.

The story so far:–
You are standing in line at the bus stop wearing your pyjamas . . .

How does it end?
(tick the box which would apply to your dream)

tick

- **1** I am late for work, I've forgotten my papers, I'm having a sneezing fit, and I have to give a speech to 150 people in French.
- **2** We're all going to a pyjama party.
- **3** My pyjama bottoms start dissolving in the rain.

The story so far:–
Something is wriggling towards you through the grass . . .

How does it end?

tick

- **1** I faint and fall towards its gaping jaws.
- **2** I identify it as the rare Brevis snake of Australia, trap it between a forked twig and claim a reward from the zoo.
- **3** I put on my sexiest underwear.

The story so far:–
On a dark road late at night you are making your way home. You hear a noise behind you . . .

How does it end?

tick

- **1** My neck freezes stiff and I cannot turn around but I hear the grunting breath growing closer as my leaden feet tread the syrupy quicksand of the road.
- **2** I put my hand out and the late night bus comes to a smart stop.
- **3** I just go on walking, ignoring Ingrid Bergman's cries, until the director yells "cut!"

The story so far:–
The train is leaving in thirty minutes and you haven't packed yet. But where are your shoes?

How does it end?

tick

- **1** The shoes are in a box which is in another box which is tied up with string which is in a bag which is chained and padlocked which is in a chest which is in a cupboard. Oh yes and my money is in my shoes.
- **2** I twist the arm of the child nearest me till it screams for mercy then I twist harder and it tells me where it's hidden them. I phone ahead, re-arrange my schedule and get the next train ten minutes later which has a discount fare.
- **3** I have hidden them. I explain sweetly to my host that I'll have to stay the night now.

The story so far:–
An evil genius has wired your vest to a nuclear device that will detonate two hundred bombs across Europe, Asia,

Russia and the Americas…

How does it end?

tick

1	The entire world perishes in a series of nuclear explosions and it's all my fault.
2	I explain to the evil genius this is a dream and vaporise him.
3	I remove my vest and all the rest of my clothes, find nearest attractive member of the requisite sex, open a bottle of champagne and spend the four minutes wisely.

The story so far:–

You are standing in your underwear washing last week's dishes with the floor rag. The doorbell rings – it's the Queen…

How does it end?

tick

1	I fall grovelling to the floor explaining I am a talking doormat.
2	I shout through the letterbox that the party's next door.
3	I explain that it's each to their own but I'm not into Queens.

The story so far:–

The wolf has you cornered, there is only one way out. You flap your arms…

How does it end?

tick

1	Slowly I lift off into the air but too slowly and the fiend seizes my ankles and I start to sink back to the ground.
2	The wolf laughs fit to bust at my Woody Allen impression and we part firm friends.
3	I get down on all fours and bite him.

ANSWERS

0-6	You are pretty normal but you weren't interested enough in this quiz to fill in the answers properly.
7-13	You are pretty normal but a bit on the ordinary side because you took this whole silly quiz bit seriously.
14-20	Possibly a little bit of a braggart are we? Boastful and a bit oversexed?
21-27	More than a bit – you're obsessed.
29-36	Absolutely ridiculous, you're wildly oversexed, and you're having two or three dreams at once. Reading too many magazine quizzes is probably the cause of your instability.

Two sheep crumb grazing

Coming out of the duvet

Hi, my name's Jake. You still awake? Well, why not just give up. Yes, go on, give it all up. I mean you've tried everything. You've tried tea, you've tried reading, you've tried reading your tea leaves. Nothing. You've tried sucking your thumb, you've tried sex, you've tried sucking your sex. Nothing again. You've re-arranged the bedclothes, tucking them in, throwing them off. You've tried breathing silently and lying still, you've tried hyperventilating and doing sit ups. It's all hopeless. Nothing works. You're still as wide awake as you were five hours ago.

So now's the time to come out of the duvet.

Why be ashamed of sleeplessness? There's nothing wrong with being awake.

15 million Australians are always awake at night. Of course there is a certain social stigma but it is the duty of all insomniacs to fight this prejudice. The time has come to stand up to be counted. Throw off your covers and say: "I'm proud to be awake!" Why be intimidated by sleepists? No, we must raise their consciousness from the slumber of ignorance, we must open their eyes to the justice of our cause. The world must be forced to see the light. Insomniacs of the world unite! You only have your duvets to lose!

Why not cut out the badges below and let the world know?

Spot the difference

There are over twenty differences between the two pictures below.
See if you can spot them.

The Great Unsheep

True peace of mind can only be yours when you grasp the fundamental sheep truth that no matter how many sheep there appear to be they are in fact all one sheep. The Great Sheep, or the Great Unsheep, for sheepness and unsheepness are of course the same.

However many sheep you count they are all part of the universal unsheep, the collective unsheep of countless legends and myths. This is the Woolly One, the All Shearing Ba from whom we all came and to whom we shall return. It is only by letting go and following the Great Unsheep that you will find peace, tranquility, fulfilment and perhaps a small amount of wool.

Repeat the mantra Baaa Baaa and focus the spirit on sheepness until you are thinking such stupid thoughts as: Am I the sheep? . . . Is the sheep me? . . . Does it matter? . . . Have I become one with the sheep? . . . Does the sheep mind? . . . Will I get arrested? Your mind is becoming one giant dip. You don't know if you are awake or asleep, the distinction is no longer important, all that matters is the Great Unsheep, the Sheepness that is all, that is everyone, the Collective Sheep, Baaaa, the sheep baaaa, what? What's all this? Blast! Nearly had you there. You were nodding off, you were nearly there.

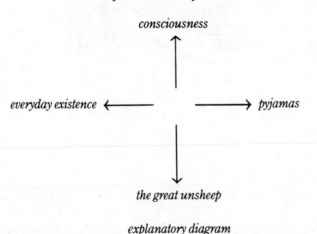

consciousness

everyday existence ← → *pyjamas*

the great unsheep

explanatory diagram

Adult Page

The next page has been rated X by the Censors Board.
Not suitable for minors.
Sensitive, puritanical killjoys may find the material offensive.

What to do
if all else fails
to send you
to sleep

(Turn page)

(continued from page 36) "... I knew that the producer of a commodity was bound to produce a use-value, to satisfy a particular social want and while the extent of those wants differed quantitively, still there existed an inner relation which settled the proportions into a regular system and that system was one of spontaneous growth and on the other hand the law and the value of commodities ultimately determined how much of its disposable working time society can expend on each particular class of commodities whatever this constant tendency to equilibrium of the various spheres of production, was exercised, only in the shape of a reaction against the constant upsetting of the equilibrium with the a-priori system on which the division of labour, within the workshop, was regularly carried out, becomes in the division of labour within the society an a-posteriori, nature imposed necessity, controlling the lawless caprice of the producers, and perceptible in the barometrical fluctuations of the market-prices with its division of labour within the workshop implying the undisputed authority of the capitalist over men that are parts of a mechanism that belong to him as the division of labour within the society brings into contact independent commodity producers, who acknowledge no other authority but that of competition, of the coercion exerted by the pressure of their mutual interests just as in the animal kingdom the 'bellum omnium contra omnes' more or less preserves the conditions of existence of every species as it does the same bourgeois mind which praises division of labour in the workshop, life long annexation of the labourer to a partial operation, and his complete subjection to capital, as being an organisation of labour that increases its productiveness – that same bourgeois mind denounces with equal vigour every conscious attempt to socially control and regulate the process of production as an inroad upon such sacred things as the rights of property, freedom and unrestricted play for the bent of the individual capitalist. "My God! It was so clear now!" he thought. "But would things look that simple in the morning?" He lay there wondering... (continued on page 76).

Sheep Walking

The 'sheep walk' is an easy and relaxing
dance step for insomniacs (see *fig 1*)

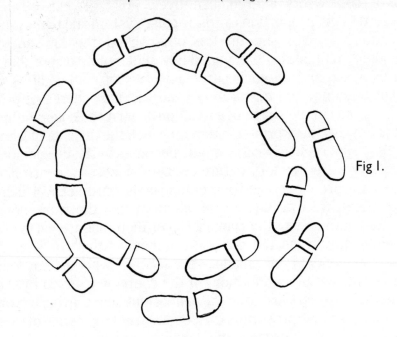

Fig 1.

It was traditionally performed with a sheep
as a partner (see *fig 2*)

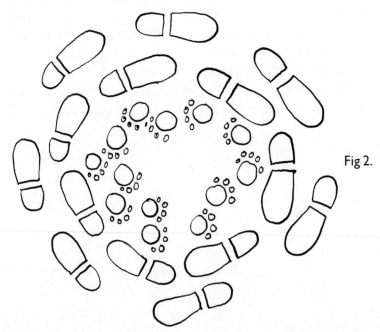

Fig 2.

The Under-the-Eye Lid World of Jacques Cousteau

Ze miracle of life! . . . Ze wonders of ze deep! All zis can be yours! . . . Simply close your eyes and nature's myriad forms will unfold before your eyes! 'Ow wonderful!

Countdown to sleep

**This is perhaps the easiest way of all to get to sleep.
Simply count back from one billion to zero. In case you
don't know how, here are the numbers:**

Nine hundred and ninety-nine thousand million, nine hundred and ninety-nine million nine hundred and ninety-nine thousand, nine hundred and ninety-nine; Nine hundred and ninety-nine thousand million, nine hundred and ninety-nine million nine hundred and ninety-nine thousand, nine hundred and ninety-eight; Nine hundred and ninety-nine thousand million, nine hundred and ninety-nine million nine hundred and ninety-nine thousand, nine hundred and ninety-seven; Nine hundred and ninety-nine thousand million, nine hundred and ninety-nine million nine hundred and ninety-nine thousand, nine hundred and ninety-six; Nine hundred and ninety-nine thousand million, nine hundred and ninety-nine million nine hundred and ninety-nine thousand, nine hundred and ninety-five; Nine hundred and ninety-nine thousand million, nine hundred and ninety-nine million nine hundred and ninety-nine thousand, nine hundred and ninety-five; Nine hundred and ninety-nine thousand million, nine hundred and ninety-nine million nine hundred and ninety-nine thousand, nine hundred and ninety-four; Nine hundred and ninety-nine thousand million, nine hundred and ninety-nine million nine hundred and ninety-nine thousand, nine hundred and ninety-three; Nine hundred and ninety-nine thousand million, nine hundred and ninety-nine million nine hundred and ninety-nine thousand, nine hundred and ninety-two; Nine hundred and ninety-nine thousand million, nine hundred and ninety-nine million nine hundred and ninety-nine thousand, nine hundred and ninety-one; Nine hundred and ninety-nine thousand million, nine hundred and ninety-nine million nine hundred and ninety-nine, nine hundred and ninety; Nine hundred and ninety-nine thousand million, nine hundred and ninety-nine million nine hundred and ninety-nine thousand, nine hundred and eighty-nine; Nine hundred and ninety-nine thousand million, nine hundred and ninety-nine million nine hundred and ninety-nine thousand, nine hundred and eighty-eight; Nine hundred and ninety-nine thousand million, nine hundred and ninety-nine million nine hundred and ninety-nine thousand, nine hundred and eighty-seven; Nine hundred and ninety-nine thousand million, nine hundred and ninety-nine milion nine hundred and ninety-nine thousand, nine hundred and eighty-six; Nine hundred and ninety-nine thousand million, nine hundred and ninety-nine million nine hundred and ninety-nine thousand, nine hundred and eighty-five; Nine hundred and ninety-nine thousand million, nine hundred and ninety-nine million nine hundred and ninety-nine thousand, nine hundred and eighty-four; Nine hundred and ninety-nine thousand million, nine hundred and ninety-nine million nine hundred and ninety-nine thousand, nine hundred and eighty-three; Nine hundred and ninety-nine thousand million, nine hundred and ninety-nine million nine hundred and ninety-nine thousand, nine hundred and eighty-two; Nine hundred and ninety-nine thousand million, nine hundred and ninety-nine million nine hundred and ninety-nine thousand, nine hundred and eighty-one; Nine hundred and ninety-nine thousand million, nine hundred and ninety-nine million nine hundred and ninety-nine

THE BIG SHEEP

2·30 AM TUESDAY — I COULDN'T SLEEP. AT THE BACK OF MY MIND SOMETHING KEPT GNAWING AWAY AT ME ABOUT LADY MARCHMARE AND THAT PHONEY STORY — BUT IF **SHE** HAD THE DIAMONDS THEN WHO KILLED JACKO — AND WHY WERE THE MOB SO INTERESTED IN LOUISE?

THERE WAS NOTHING ELSE FOR IT — I'D JUST **HAVE** TO FINISH THE BOOK. ..... I WAS RIGHT ABOUT LADY MARCHMARE — SHE WAS BEING BLACKMAILED BY JACKO WHEN LOUISE..

SUDDENLY I HEARD THE SOUND OF SHATTERING GLASS —

CRASH!

SOMEBODY'D THROWN A HOT WATER BOTTLE THROUGH MY WINDOW — ON IT WAS A NOTE THAT SMELLED OF PERFUME

OUTSIDE THE BAR I PULLED MY DUVET UP ROUND MY NECK AND HOPED NO ONE WOULD RECOGNISE ME —

NEEDN'T HAVE BOTHERED — IT WAS ONE OF THOSE FANCY NEW JOINTS WITH HUMPHREY BOGART ALL OVER THE WALLS

...L THE BARS IN ALL ...WORLD, I HAD TO ...INTO **THIS** ONE!

BOGEY WOGEY?

OH YA SUPER!

IT HAD TO BE HER — I SHOWED HER THE WATER BOTTLE AND SHE SMILED AND SPOKE....

.. KINDA SOFT AND CLASSY..

WHEN GREAT SLEEPWALKERS CURL THEIR TOES, THERE'S ALWAYS SOMEONE THERE TO PICK THE STUFFING OUT OF THE MATTRESS

I COULD TELL THIS WAS NO ORDINARY BROAD — BUT IT SLOWLY DAWNED ON ME THAT I DIDN'T KNOW WHAT THE **HELL** SHE WAS TALKING ABOUT. I DECIDED TO KEEP COOL AND PLAY **HER** GAME

..WHEN NIGHT FALLS, NO OYSTER WILL BARK AT THE MOON

IT SEEMED TO WORK — SHE TOOK OUT **ANOTHER** HOT WATER BOTTLE, SWAPPED IT WITH MINE AND THEN VANISHED..

THE MINUTE I GOT OUT I FOUND MYSELF BEING BUNDLED INTO A CAR —

THE NEXT THING I KNOW, SOME MOBSTER IS STARING AT ME FROM THE OTHER SIDE OF A DESK..

WE'RE LOOKING FOR SOMETHING BARLOWE — IT'S WARM AND SNUG LIKE A KANGEROO'S POUCH AND IT'S FULL OF **HOT WATER**

THINGS WERE GOING TO GET ROUGH UNLESS I ACTED **FAST** — I HAD AN IDEA — IT WAS A LONG SHOT BUT IT **MIGHT** WORK....

I MADE A RUN FOR IT! AT THE DOOR A HAT STAND TRIED TO STOP ME AND PUT UP A FIGHT — SOON A LAMP SHADE HAD JOINED IN —

I GOT AWAY — BUT THEY CHASED ME DOWN THE STREET —

PING

FINALLY, I MANAGED TO SHAKE 'EM OFF ~

BEN
L

FORTUNATELY, A LATE NIGHT KANGEROO WAS GOING MY WAY SO I TOOK A RIDE

MY SECRETARY WAS UP LATE PLAYING A MOZART CONCERTO ON HER TYPE-WRITER —

I THREW MYSELF ON THE BED AND TOOK OUT THE WATER BOTTLE ~

SUDDENLY THE ROOM WAS FULL OF HOODLUMS ~

WE **FORGOT** SOMETHING, BARLOWE

WE'VE COME TO KISS YOU **GOODNIGHT!**

E LEANED OVER AND GAVE ME A G **SUGARY WET** SMACKER — THEN HEY ALL TROUPED OUT!

I EMPTIED THE BOTTLE ONTO THE FLOOR — IT WAS FULL OF **DIAMONDS!**

SUDDENLY IT ALL BECAME CLEAR TO ME — THE DIAMONDS — THE MOB — — LOUISE! — I MUST HAVE DRIFTED OFF ON CHAPTER EIGHT AND DREAMT THE WHOLE THING UP —

ANOTHER CASE SOLVED ~ I FIGURED LOUISE WOULD BE ALONG SOON TO PICK UP HER HOT WATER BOTTLE . . . . .

ROGER PLANER

Mr and Mrs Goodnight

This is Mr and Mrs Goodnight This is their son Johnny And this is their little dog Spot The Goodnights all live in a house on a hill Mr and Mrs Goodnight are very good. At 8 o'clock every night they go upstairs to bed and go straight to sleep Johnny is good too. He always goes straight to bed when he is told And so does Spot The Goodnights are always happy and smiling because they always get plenty of sleep And they always get plenty of sleep because they never worry about anything. When Mr and Mrs Goodnight hear about something worrying they just say 'hey ho, no point worrying about it' and go to sleep. And so does Johnny And so does Spot

This is Mr Jumbly He's an axe-wielding maniac. And this is his axe One day Mr Jumbly breaks into the Goodnight's house while they are fast asleep and kills them all, horribly Hey ho. If they'd been awake like me, worrying about axe wielding maniacs, it might never have happened. The End.

What do you mean 'the story is unfair?'... It serves them right the SMUG BASTARDS! I CAN'T STAND people like that who can just go to sleep at the drop of a hat and are always so BRIGHT AND CHEERFUL in the morning... THEY MAKE ME SICK!! And anyway... It's MY STORY and I can do what I like with it!

Revenge

**This is a game you can play all by yourself.
It usually lasts for 25–45 minutes.**

The rules are simple:

First, think of someone whose fault it is you're in this state. It could be a friend, colleague or relative. But it must be their fault you are this sleepless, sweating, pathetic, self-pitying lump of uselessness.

Now think of a suitable revenge.

Examples

1. How about booking them an early morning alarm call – now.

2. Or phone the fire brigade and have three screaming fire engines sent round.

3. Go round to their house and put a '25 pints please' note on their door. While you're there you could put a dog turd in an envelope, light it, push it through the letter box and ring the bell. Hang around to watch as they come storming down and stamp the fire out.

4. Why not shave off all their hair, cover them with motor oil and make them watch Starsky and Hutch?

5. Or best of all – become dictator of Greenland and get an army of stormtroopers to invade their street, tie them up and threaten to vaporise them unless they say they're sorry a hundred times and that you're the greatest and everything is all right and you can go to sleep.

Games Sheep Play:
Stickers on the windscreen

Famous Sheep Jokes....

Customer: Do you sell sheep wool?
Shopkeeper: If they've got the money I'll serve anyone.

Last time little Sam went to the zoo he got into trouble for feeding the sheep. He fed them to the tigers.

What do the Australians call baby sheep?
Lambs

Doctor, doctor! I feel like a sheep!
That's baaaad.

What's white, woolly, has four legs and is found in Manhattan?
A lost sheep.

Frightened of sleeping at night? Terrified of dying in bed? Why be a slave to mortality when for just a few pounds a week you can sleep soundly in the knowledge of eternal life? Because that's what we at Re Inc are offering – guaranteed Re-incarnation at a price every family can afford.

Yes, you too can come back from the dead. No longer the secret of Pharaohs and Peruvian Indians, re-incarnation has now been scientifically proved and is available on easy-to-pay terms for the upwardly mobile. Nu Life's fully comprehensive service combines the wisdom of the East with the technology of the West to guarantee you the chance to start with a clean slate.

You can choose from over ten different lives to suit your pocket and aspirations. Our Budget Special offers the chance to return as a chartered surveyor for just £8.95 a week* (*subject to floating exchange rate), while for just £3 more you could be a fridge salesman or, for only £14.95 a TV game host.

For those with grander ambitions we have our Golden Return. How about PM of a developing country (£38.50, subject to IMF restrictions), or Grand Prix Racing Driver (£52.95)? Perhaps you'd really like to splash out and book a minor aristocrat. We even have a few places left on our Corgi Special. We can't say more! Phone us for a quote.

Whichever Nu Life you choose you can rest assured Re Inc will always be there to help. All our sales staff are re-incarnated *as* sales staff and will continue to serve you through the ages.

So why not buy a good night's sleep *and* eternal life by clipping the coupon below. There's no obligation and no salesman will call. But hurry - remember what the Bible says: there are the quick and the dead; you definitely want to be the quick!

New for Old!!!

Please rush me your Nu Life for Old Information pack. I am under 82

Name: ....

Address: ....

....

Current Incarnation: ....

Desired Re-incarnation: ....

d to: Re Inc
Pen 76
Milton Keynes

Take Sheep

Here's an interesting new game for film enthusiasts.
(Who also like sheep)

Citizen Sheep
It's a Mad Mad Mad Mad Sheep
For Your Sheep Only
The Sound of Sheep
All Quiet on the Western Sheep
All Sheep on the Western Front
Gone With the Sheep
El Sheep
Sheep over the River Kwai
Sheep flew over the Cuckoo's Nest
The Sheep Hunter
Everything you wanted to know about Sheep
but were afraid to ask
Mr Hulot's Sheep
Sheep

What about Sheep Two?
Sheep Three and Sheep Four?
Now Try Some Yourself

What's new…?
Annie…
How to Marry a…

That's the idea – – –
Think Adventure,
Romance, Danger

Raiders of the Lost…
Around the…in Eighty Days
The Third…

Who was in that?
Oh yes I remember, it
was Orson Sheep…
Or was it Douglas
Sheep Junior?

The Sheep of Baghdad
A Sheep too Far
Cat on a Hot tin Sheep
The Magnificent Sheep
Butch Cassidy and the Sundance Sheep

And here's something
a bit more arty
for the real sheep
Buffs. Foreign Classics

Ivan the Sheep
Alexander the Sheep
The Three Sheep
The Seven Sheep
Le 400 Sheep

"Frankly my dear, I
couldn't give a sheep"
Here is a space for
your own suggestions

....
....
....
....
....
....
....
....
....
....
....
....

Passing the time No 23

Exploring the body

Why not visit all those parts of your body you usually ignore and pass over in the hurley-burly of everyday life? Think how many interesting byways and backwaters there are in your body which you usually don't give a second glance to! Well, now's the chance to explore these little known hideouts in the depth they deserve. After all, God created us in his image and if we wish to know him fully we must also know ourselves.

For example, have you ever taken a really good look at your armpit? Oh, no doubt you've felt it from time to time, as you unceremoniously wash it out and perhaps spray it with some toxic chemicals. Some people even remove its natural undergrowth. But have you ever taken a good, hard look at it? What an extraordinary piece of the body the armpit is! Without it

your whole arm would fall off and you wouldn't have stained shirts, in fact you probably wouldn't have shirts at all, but a sort of cut off smock.

Then there's the navel. What a useful little storehouse! Not only does it quite automatically create its own lint, but it can store oil, honey and even Typex liquid for those really intimate moments. It can also be made into a mouth with an imaginative touch of lipstick and, of course, can be comtemplated for hours without becoming bored.

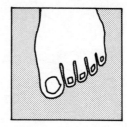

How about the space between your toes? These little understood details offer hours of endless amusement. Hold pens in them and write to Aunty May, or use to paint minimalist pictures. Try smoking a cigarette between the toes or even making a cream tea.

Simple models to build in bed No 34

THE ZEPPELIN

What You Need:

49 matchsticks
Sticky back plastic
An old squeezy bottle
Four thousand square metres best quality linen
Hot air
Rubber solution glue

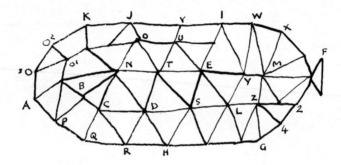

What to Do

1) Take the 49 matchsticks and, with the sticky back plastic
... you haven't got the matchsticks?

2) Get the matches.

3) Right. Ready now? Good. Take the matchsticks
and make a frame round the squeezy bottle.

4) Now take the four thousand square metres of linen and carefully
stretch it round ... you haven't got that? You didn't get the matches
either, did you? Look, how seriously are you taking this? I really don't see
why I should bother telling how to make a Zeppelin if you can't even be
bothered to get the simple household materials. No, I'm sorry. You're
clearly not committed. What sort of insomniac are you anyway? Quite
frankly you can't even be bothered to get out of bed, can you? You're not
serious about this. And you've wasted all that hot air. You're already
getting sleepy! Go on, off you go back to page 24, and don't come back
here till you're really awake!

The Bedtime Look

by our Fashion Editor
Styling Moose

Your Moose on the loose has been out and about checking out what lambs nationwide are wearing and daring in fields up and down the country. The good news is that the all over wool look is back! Gone is the shawn and cheerful style of last Spring. Wild and woolly is back! The sheepwalks of Paris are crammed with the new full-fleece line – they may call us mutton but sure as barbed-wire hurts the froggies have style! Well, heads are turning when it comes to sheepcuts. Last year it was enough to just cut it short and close, but now the cool sheep can choose from over twenty style sensations. So next time you visit your shearer ask him to try one of the following and be the coolest sheep in the pen.

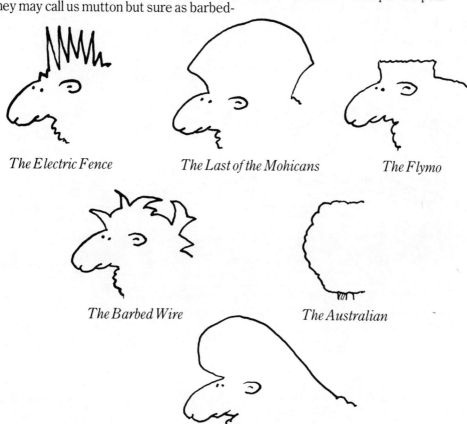

The Electric Fence

The Last of the Mohicans

The Flymo

The Barbed Wire

The Australian

The Hound Dog

Pillow Talk IV

It's 4.45 on Tuesday morning and Sam and Suzie are still having their chat. See if you can help them out again.

How to use this book to really really get to sleep

If the last idea didn't work here's one that the publishers guarantee.

1. Close the book.

2. Hold the book in the right hand.

3. Extend your right arm.

4. Bring the book sharply up and hit yourself on the head as hard as possible.

Repeat until unconscious.

Reviews

"I could hardly lift it up." *The Morning After*

"Should fill a gap under the door." *FT*

"I liked it a lot." *Goofy*

"Real gripping stuff – I was on the edge of my bed. Yawn? I thought we'd never start!" *Philip Duvet*

"One of those books you can't help putting down." *The Bed Post*

"I could hardly wait to switch the light off." *The Morning Reveille*

"Combines the wit of the Marx Brothers, the suspense of Hitchcock with the insight of Wittgenstein." *Elsie Karamazov*